GN00789605

MUTTERINGS OF A CHAR

Words and drawings by

PAM BROWN

≣EXLEY

First published in Great Britain by Exley Publications Ltd.,
16 Chalk Hill, Watford, Herts WD1 4BN.
© Pam Brown 1984
British Library Cataloguing in Publication Data
Brown, Pam
 The mutterings of a char.
 1. Domestics — England
 I. Title
 640'.46'0924   HD8039.D52G7
 ISBN 1-85015-014-1
All rights reserved. No part of this publication may be
reproduced or transmitted in any form or by any means,
electronic or mechanical, including photocopy, recording,
or any information storage and retrieval system without
permission in writing from the publisher.

Printed and bound in Great Britain by Hazell Watson and
Viney Limited, member of BPCC Group, Aylesbury, Bucks.

Introduction

Real life, mercifully, rarely comes concentrated, and a char's existence is more boredom than event. Embarrassment and hurt being far from my purpose, I have boiled down the bones of experience to make what I hope is a sort of Scotch Broth. In the process the ladies I have known have, inevitably, run together.

Over the years I have worked for alarming ladies, cunning ladies, drooping and doleful ladies, hysterical, tipsy, giggly and just plain stupid ladies. Some have driven me spare - as probably I have them - but hardly one of them didn't have her good side.

The usual lady, however, is, quite simply, kind and friendly and considerate, and scarcely ever forgets to leave out one's money, or to scrape the spaghetti off the dinner plates. But, alas, kindness and friendliness and consideration make for monotonous reading.

So let us concentrate on The Others.

Pam Brown

3

Char Lady

There *are* women who simply love cleaning other people's houses. I've not *met* any, but ...

An interesting social ploy is to keep a completely straight face — or a gentle, slightly superior smile — when asked at a party What Does One Do. And say one is a Charlady. And then sit back and watch them disentangle their expression.

Cleaning woman, Daily, Lady-who-comes-in, Domestic, Treasure — a char by any other name still smells of bleach.

Note to single men: Ladies who 'do', don't. If they did, they would have.

Many a char wishes she dare. The money is better and it's over quicker.

Chars are like nannies — they can produce Awful Examples from their experience of previous employers. Naming No Names.

The cheating char sprays the air with polish just before she leaves, half an hour early.

A cleaner is someone who knows how much of you is you, and how much is the Librium in the bathroom cabinet.

A char is a vacuum cleaner that is unfortunately capable of recognising, and analysing, human detritus.

A char lives off cuts of meat her Missus hasn't even heard of.

There comes a time when a nice little man at a party will swear he's seen you before — and you will tell him that you are the Daily Woman. He is usually enchanted. His wife's voice shoots up a full octave and she switches to the voice she uses at her Oxfam committee.

A char's duty is to soothe the guilt complexes of the women who employ her to do the jobs they feel they should be able to manage alone.

The char is the marooned housewife's cut-rate psychiatrist. And *she* does house calls.

A char works not with inanimate objects but with the projection of her employer's dream. God help her if she chips it.

It's an odd fact that ancient Greek civilization rested squarely on the slave.
Odder that Women's Liberation rests squarely on the char.

Everyone spends their time cleaning up after someone else, rectifying emotional, educational, physical, monetary and psychological mistakes.
I just clean up straightforward dirt.

There is a marvellous satisfaction in the comparison of the house you are about to leave with the house you entered three hours previously.
There is no satisfaction at all in confronting it all again the next morning.

I think lazy housewives get handed a mop when they present themselves at the gates of Heaven. Chars get a cup of tea and a Chocolate Digestive.

No char can make up her mind whether it's worse to clean a house that doesn't need cleaning — or one where *no-one* else ever cleans a thing.

Women are battling to give their sisters equal opportunities with men and to widen their horizons and their skills. If they succeed they will end up having to do their own housework.

Mutterings

Being a char is rather like having your children small again. You can be very fond of your employers, while deploring their habits.

The guests see the buffet. The char sees the preparation. She's generally very *glad* she wasn't invited.

A char doesn't covet much that you've got.

Your char would rather have the price of a bottle of Chanel than a bottle of Chanel.

Meaty chicken carcasses in the bin come under the heading of Cruelty to Chars.

Employers always seem shocked when they come home unexpectedly and find their char listening to a radio play as they iron. Presumably they feel they have hired *all* faculties.

A char is not so much an employee as a possession.

Charring is brushing down chairs you don't curl up in, making beds you don't cuddle down into, washing plates you don't eat off and cleaning up after parties you didn't attend. It's rather like sex by correspondence.

Chars may fume over your diabolical vacuum cleaner, growl into your gas oven, breathe heavily over the state of your bath — but in any emergency They Are On Your Side.

No, your char will *not* try to do the upstairs windows both sides. Whatever you say about pivots.

In these days of easy wash, easy iron, status lies in pure cotton, pure linen, pure silk, hand-made lace and a char who is mug enough to iron it all.

Chars should not be expected to empty mousetraps. Your mouse. Your trap. Your problem.

Never judge your char by *her* house. By the time she gets home, she's too bloody tired to do her *own* housework.

A char being shown round your beautiful home for the first time is reducing everything you have to a cleaning problem.

You can become *very* good friends with your Missis — but you can still hate her drains.

Chars bleed too. Check your Elastoplast.

The char who tries to do everything on the list ends up with a longer list.

A wise mistress knows she's employing a fat, elderly lady of a fairly nervous disposition — not Superwoman.

Back to work

My dear. There you are. Are you all right now? Good. I'm so glad
— the ironing has been simply piling up and I've not had a
second to touch it.
It's incongruous, isn't it, we should both be ill at the same time.
My dear, *agony*. Absolute agony. I've had Masterson round *every*
day. *Complete* bed rest. But you know me. I can't just *lie* there. I
simply have to be up and doing. I'd *creep* down and get on with
my little water colour ... one can't just lie abed, can one? Have
you seen it? Yes. It is coming along rather nicely.
Oh, thank you, yes. I'd like you to tackle those cupboards first.
Sheer chaos. I just toss everything in — you know me! Look,
stand on this chair. It's far the steadiest. I think if you stretch a
little you should be able to do the top shelf nicely. Yes, they *are* a
little heavy, but just get one down at a time.
Now, I must pop upstairs and be a good girl and take my pill.
Then I'll just do a little weeding. Masterson says I should try to
get a little fresh air *every* day.
Oh, you can't come on Thursday. Oh dear. Well that *is* a pity, I've
a dinner party and I really did want the entire place *glittering*.
You couldn't put it off until Friday. Oh, it's booked. Oh well,
these hospitals,they are *all* the same. Though it seems very *soon*
to have a check up, doesn't it.
After all,you've only been out a week!

Ditties and Digs

A sordid old man of Cawmpore
threw his beer cans all over the floor,
stacked his plates in the sink
and said with a wink
"What else is a charwoman for?"

. . . .

Hey diddle diddle, the lad's on the fiddle
the bank and larder are bare
but there's plenty of booze
and they're off on a cruise
leaving me with the kids and au pair

. . . .

Ring a ring o' roses, a pocket full of pot,
Gerda in the attic and Justin in the cot.
Me to do the dishes,
John to do the yard.
The Missis says that Taxes make existence very hard.

. . . .

It's not a matter of self deprecation
to say I find it hard to think
of Higher Things when gazing down a sink:
I lack the gift of sublimation.

. . . .

Missis is furious today
He didn't book their holiday
- which means they'll have to give up Spain
and go to bloody Greece again.

The Morning After

Oh Ho — we've had a dinner party. And we're *terribly* sorry about the mess are we. Like hell we are. What did we have, now. Oh, yukky, yukky yuk. Unsuccessful Potage for starters. Make a nice wallcovering in the hall. Eau de petits pois. And fish. Oh, we *were* going it. In a spiced sauce. Bit odd after that soup, but one sees her point. I remember the fish. How she *dared* ... I *must* keep an eye on 'The Times' obituaries over the next few days. Ambitious. Veau en papillottes. My God, they had to fight for it, didn't they? *Welded*. Still, they appear to have prized at least some of it free. Water ices. My dear — my very own Italian recipe. As purchased from Tesco last Friday. Still, served with elegance and candles it could have looked rather splendid. And he's bound to have laid on enough booze to have blunted, at least, the worst of it. Yes, there they are — the stack of dead men. A vivacious little wine we picked up in the Loire. And if you'll believe *that* ... I wonder if she told the story of her Maharajah proposing by moonlight ... Bless her heart, she does tell it very prettily — all white arms and Marks and Spencer bangles and Kohl. Now, stop being bitchy. You know you love that blue see-through dress. And it's no good thinking how nice it would be if she handed it on to you. You've nothing left to show through it. Still, at least you *can* cook, dear. Come to think of it, maybe next time I *could* cook ... No, she'd never allow it. Successful Woman Novelist Does Not Allow Success To Interfere With Her Role As Housewife and Mother. Oh Ho.

Happy Homecoming, Madam

Tell me once again of Rio,
lentemente or con brio,
moan to me of all the pain
incurred in travelling by plane.
Grouse about the caviar
and, dear Madam, I, your char
will leave you to unpack,
wash up and take the empties back
and cope with all the aftermath
of your impromptu Welcome Home
- the lipstick on the telephone,
the diamante-studded shoe
stuck firmly in the downstairs loo,
the glasses in the bath.

For Duty Free does not suffice
to balance out congealing rice
and ash trays full of olive stones
and bits of quiche and chicken bones.
And so, my tanned and weary friend,
don't tempt your char to make an end
of her engagement; not until
she's cleared the shelves and window sill
and hoovered up the nuts.
Believe me, bottles of Arpège,
do nothing, Madam, to assuage
the grinding in her guts.

And there are still the Harrods frocks
you draggled over sand and rocks,
to wash and iron, and all his shirts
enlivened by exotic dirts
- Tequila sunrise, pepper sauce
- and damned Ambre Solaire, of course.

12

Remember, Madam, that your char
can be pushed an inch or two too far
And, Madam,though I sympathise
with all your tales - and all your lies
of High Romance in foreign clime
- dear Madam
I HAVE NOT THE TIME

The Scrubber

If I were young and thinner,
rather than deal with your disgusting last night's dinner
I think I'd much prefer to be a sinner
and walk the streets:
But I am old and sagging
and, having dealt with that congealing mass, I'm dragging
the Hoover round your lounge. Admittedly I'm flagging,
but there are fitted sheets
to iron, and sixteen shirts and half a dozen dresses
and then your children's individual messes
to tidy up;
your bright peroxide tresses
to hook out of the drain.
My dear employer, yours may be the brain
position, looks - but you give me a PAIN . . .
And yet I'll come again
and yet again,
plodding through snow or sleet or hurricane,
for, after coffee and a slice of bread and honey,
and picking up the money,
I shall go home and soak my tired feet
- and then I'll see the whole damned thing as funny
and so remain
comparatively sane.
(And, after all, a whore
may find her *job a bore)*

Going Up

My town is a seed bed for young social climbers, couples with
eyes fixed firmly on a seat on the Board. When they first move
into the district there seems still to be a touch of tender green
about them, but the moment that the vital promotion comes
through, their tenuous roots are wrenched up and they depart to
harden off in richer soil, under a more burning sun. They are
civil enough neighbours, but rarely around, for their spare time
is largely spent in making useful contacts, an occupation which
forces them to employ elderly ladies who will undertake the
household chores.

Odd. My first pair of young executives on the way up have no
faces. I presume that at the time I could have recognised them in
the street but, then, of course, young executives do not use
streets a great deal, save to roar down in their sleek, but wholly
respectable cars.

They had, surprisingly, a child. Set against their bounding
youthfulness he seemed almost elderly, the victim of a trick of
Time. He had obviously been a mistake, but was made the best
of, being a living, breathing prestige object. He was run to his
small, exclusive school each morning in the car, there to receive
a woefully inadequate education in the company of boys with
valuable connections. His father would have preferred a
boarding school, but as his own life style hung by a singularly
slender thread, from which the fees of even the most minor
school would have torn him, he settled for St Pierre's private day
school.

Theirs was a moderately priced semi-detached neo-Georgian
residence, a spring-board to better things. My bungalow was the
blotch on an otherwise respectable road, unpainted, the haunt
of cats. However, perhaps for Clive there was a touch of The
Poor Man At His Gate about it, a shadow of forelocks and lodges.
At any rate, I was always within reach if I was needed. And
needed I was.

"Sorry to come banging on your door so very early, Mrs B. Were
you in the bath? Oh, I really am *so* sorry, but we have to go to
Henley. *Now.* Totally unexpected telephone call from Robert.
Mr Miles. Patrick's in the house on his own, *terribly* spotty and
hot. I'd be so grateful if you could just pop over and keep an eye

15

on him. I'll leave the phone number in case he gets worse. Isn't it *incredible* how they always do something like this when one has an engagement? Of course, if you're the least worried, do phone Dr Habib. Patrick's friend, Roger, was coming about four. I suppose it will be all right. Do shoo him away if not. Might take Patrick's mind off the spots. If he *does* stay, perhaps you could just scratch up some tea for them? I *must* fly. Oh dear, you're shivering. Do get inside, Mrs B. We can't have *you* ill, *can* we?" Money was never mentioned. A clutch of hands and one would be left with a little squodge of notes in one's palm, which one could examine after the car had gone. Not a very large squodge. I thought of my dear Aunt in Pimlico who suffered similarly, and happily, at the beck and call of Arabs. Thick white envelopes containing what looked like newly-printed currency. Most courteous gratitude. And a taxi home.

I really did not see a great deal of them. Neither did Patrick. There was the hang-gliding and the squash, the badminton and golf, the epeés among the umbrellas, the scuba gear dripping in the bathroom, the boules bought in a moment of Gallic insanity, the croquet set laid down against a more affluent future.The equipment was part of the investment and the more interesting items were left carelessly where any visitor would spot them. *House and Garden, Vogue, Tatler* and *The Field* filled much the same role. *The Sun* was under the sofa cushions.

They moved, at last, with their fencing masks, their badminton racquets and their golf trophies. Perhaps one of the stock exchange tips had come good.

The next couple were of sterner stuff. No children, no intention of children. They were bound for the heights, and *fast*. Much the same records as their predecessors — the complete Beethoven symphonies and racks of 'background' discs to hum away below the decibels of party talk. A bathroom that smelled like Selfridges ground floor. A dressing table thick with Givenchy. No books, no objets trouvé. No time. And consequently, no epeés, no scuba gear, no deck shoes.

Cleaning was mundane. No surprises. 'The Perfumed Garden' and the 'Kama Sutra' by the bed. Nail clippings in the deep pile carpets. The sheets were rather more depressing than those of the last couple as having decided against children, they had decided for dogs. I would, I think, have expected poodles or one of the wilder new varieties, but was confronted by two

16

outrageous mongrels, shaggy beyond description, sloppy,
neurotic and sad. They smelled of dog and perfume and they
slept on the bed, which was thick with dog hair and patterned
with paw marks. Their names were Buck and Fizz, and they
could do very little wrong. The small section of their owners'
hearts that had not been made over to the pursuit of success,
was theirs.
This sentiment did not, of course, interfere in any way with the
active lives of their owners. All day the dogs stayed in the locked
house, sitting half way up the stairs where they could watch the
door. My key in the lock sent them into a hysteria of joy and they
lovingly supported every move I made, including the attempt to
remove their fur from the stair carpet.

The couple belonged — to almost everything. The Conservative Club, the Round Table, Luncheon Clubs. Anywhere they could meet people of the right sort. In the summer, lunacy set in. The dinner parties and predictable dances over, they hurled themselves into gaiety. Fun suppers began. All about the dull little town would race the garage polished cars; soup here, fondue there, le pouding somewhere else: Madly gay. An evocation of the twenties without the sparkle, and none of the participants quite as young as they thought they were.

I got the washing up, of course. Never keep a dog and bark oneself. I got the ash trays and the spat out olives and the cigarette stubs in the plant pots, the wine stains on the linen and the lipstick on the towels. The splashes in the loo.

And the dogs.

The parting of the ways came abruptly. I was admittedly a little weary of the set-up, but it was convenient, I needed the money and the dogs were on my conscience. It was the dogs who pulled the structure down about our ears. I let myself in on a clear spring day, greeted the two madly whirling bozos and moved into the living room, when I discovered that someone had accidentally shut the kitchen door. The dogs, shut out from the layers of newspaper that, God knows, had been hard enough to take, had been forced to use the living room carpet. They must have either felt guilty, or euphoric, as they had employed the length and breadth of the room. I gave a last pat to their gormless, shaggy heads and left, never to return.

They moved, all of them, to a bigger, better house in Surrey, where they could 'entertain more friends and live a fuller life' with, presumably, even more empty bedrooms and unfilled cupboards.

With their departure I found myself my last climbing couple, who proved at last that one can climb and remain happily human. They appeared to be taking a rather less precipitous route, sign-posted with examinations and with pauses to admire the scenery.

The very ordinary house I took on changed slowly and steadily with the passing months. Somehow, between work and examinations, birthday parties and cut-price skiing, they found the time and energy to transform it, plastering and tiling, stitching and panelling and wiring, scrubbing up and sanding down, potting and pruning and pricking out. Their amiable,

18

mindless Persian sat in the middle of it, exuding a rather blurred affection for all mankind.

Molly and Bill. Their friends were of their age and not in the least Important. Yet. A few naughty books sat among the Catherine Cookson's and the Insurance manuals, but there was an odd air of innocence about them, the happy air of children playing house. No one ever forgot anyone's birthday, or anniversary, or move, or promotion. There were always cards on the fireplace busy with bunnies and kisses and little bees with flowers behind their ears.

They made me feel very old, very fat, very shabby and very lazy, this bushy tailed set — but with no urge whatever to emulate their lifestyle. It seemed to me as I ran my eye down the crammed engagement calenders in the kitchen that it was all far harder than cleaning loos.

The Interview

"Do please come through to the lounge. Now, as you'll see, we've a *huge* house and I do *need* somebody. My husband and I have a *great* many social and civic duties and I want to feel I have someone I can really *trust*. Could you give me references? It really is so very difficult to judge by appearances these days. You *look* splendid, of course ..."

"Oh yes, if you need them. Though for three hours a week ..."

"Ah, but you see, I am *surrounded* by beautiful and *rare* things. I *live* for beautiful things. The crystal swan: the porcelain flowers: the *exquisite* figurines. Capo di Monte. I must feel sure they are treated with really *loving* care. Could you *cope?*"

"You mean, wash them?"

"Oh, I'll leave you the *exact* details and all the necessary equipment. And then there's the silver. Baroque, you know. Well, baroque *style,* that is, of course."

"Of course."

"You *know* silver. Well then, I could feel easy there. *No* polish left in the crannies, eh! *Now.* There are six bedrooms and even when I haven't visitors, I like them all to be done thoroughly every week. No skimping under beds. The last woman was *very* skimpy under beds. The boys' rooms *are* inclined to be a little chaotic, but you'll just have to burrow your way through, won't you? Boys! Still, we wouldn't have them any different, *would* we?"

"The master bedroom — *as* you will see, there is a *great* deal of glass. Faced wardrobes you know. The *entire* wall. I really am *very* fussy about glass. And it is possible, as I am sure you know, to get an immaculate, *glittering* finish without resort to chemicals. And, of course, the windows. Right through the house, that is. I only expect you to do outside downstairs, except, of course, for those directly above the extension. That gives a *splendidly* solid roof to stand on. You just *pop* out of the window!

"In *here,* as you see, the suite *is* velvet. I really do insist that it is done thoroughly *every* week. I *am* a little naughty with my petit point so be *very* careful about needles! The usual dusting and polishing and vacuum cleaning. And the parquet — I do have an *excellent* old polisher, and that, of course, copes with the hall too. *So* welcoming, a really mirror-like floor to greet one as one comes through the door!

"The kitchen. Ah. Now, in the kitchen everything is *very* easy to keep *really* nice. I must say I am *very* proud of my kitchen. French Farmhouse. Tiles. But I don't want them *touched* with cleaners. Hot water and elbow grease, that's my recipe. And a quarry tiled floor. *Beautiful.* Now those, I am sure you'll agree, cannot be skimped — a real down-on-the-knees job. The dear old stove, of *course.* I'm afraid that's often in a *little* bit of a pickle as my sons *will* make themselves snacks at *all* hours! So, of course, you'll often be confronted by a *lot* of washing up.

"The drains *do* give a little trouble — I'm afraid you'll have to poke away with the old wire sometimes — the boys again. And they really are *naughty* in the bathroom. And sometimes it looks as if there had been a *snow*storm of Monsieur Houbigant talc — and they just *abandon* the bath.

"The stairs I like done *first* with the stiff brush and pan and *then* with the vacuum cleaner. The carpets *are* a problem with Itsie and Bitzie. Pedigree, you know. *Snow* white Persians. It means a wet cloth and a real *rub.* It looks appalling otherwise on the indigo pile. Now, there's *no* need to try and memorize all this. Every week I'll leave you a really long, absolutely *detailed* list. I shan't expect you to cope with everything, of course. *I* take *complete* charge of the pot plants and Albert insists that he cleans his own trophies. Golf, you know. A great golfer.

"Oh — and I *shall* expect you to clean out the goldfish once in a while. I simply can't bear to touch them. Silly me!

"And if either of the cats is sick — and they have *very* delicate little tummies — you're not to worry. I keep a special bucket and disinfectant under the stairs.

"I feel sure that *if* the references are satisfactory we will suit *very* well. I'm offering 75p an hour and the old lady who was here before you — she *died,* poor dear — found the entire arrangement *very* satisfactory.

"Oh, *careful* of Boojie. Did I mention Boojie? Down! Down Boy! *Pure* bred poodle — a little snappy, but if you are patient … Now, all this brass … Mrs. Brown?

"How strange. Maybe she was taken ill … Mrs Brown! MRS BROWN! Silly woman's left her umbrella."

21

The Nineteen Eighties

In the early days of Victoria an employer of servants knew where she was. God had, after all, put her there, just as he had put Bessie and Annie and Jane below stairs with the black beetles and the scullery sink. They were another species, a rung on the ladder of creation, owing fealty to their mistress as she owed fealty to her bearded and respectable deity. But with the departure of the living-in-maid-of-all-work and the consequent rise of the Daily, the ordered universe collapsed in ruins.

In the early years, of course, the years celebrated by Agatha Christie and Noel Coward, the years when she was known as The Daily Woman, she was still recognisable as having swung down from another branch of the Darwinian tree from that of her mistress. She wore a hat indoors for one thing and brought her apron with her. She called her employer Mum and was a Character, like as not. Friendly and competent — but she knew Her Place. And said so, frequently. She was grateful for left-overs and vanished into working class oblivion at the end of the day.

It didn't last long. The hat went first. The modern employer is left with only a shadow of her former authority — and the images of departed Treasures in the pages of reprinted detective stories — for, with a jolt and a rumble, the two stratas collapsed in upon one another, to leave employer and employee in eyeball-to-eyeball confrontation.

Your current Daily probably lives just up the road, or, worse, she arrives in her own car. It is difficult to give orders to someone whose car seems to be running a great deal better than your own. And whom you bumped into in the changing rooms at C and A last week in your petticoats. Hers had lace insets. You have a nasty suspicion that she does not like the tea you use, either, ever since you heard her discussing blends with the assistant in the chic little specialist shop you thought you had discovered. She is courteous, admittedly, and she *does* clean behind the loo and do out the drains and wash up the breakfast things and get a splendid shine on the parquet. But you have to stop yourself apologising for reading Mills and Boone romances — it's something about the way she stacks them on the bedside table. You wonder what *she* reads. Freud?

She's charming, of course. Helpful. But it *was* a bit disconcerting when she gave you a couple of addresses in Rome last holiday. What in Heaven's name did she *do* before she came to you? And why is she doing it now? Perhaps she's the look-out for a gang of jewel thieves. Though with a diamond solitaire and a flaked opal pendant as the take, it would scarcely seem worth her trouble. If she wore a cap and apron, had adenoids, slept in the attic, you could be kind and interested and give brisk, sensible orders. The mistresses in books seemed to gain considerable kudos from asking after their chars poor bad legs. Your char's legs look splendid. You have a sneaking feeling that it's *you* that would have any poor, bad leg that was going — and that she would have the address of an excellent osteopath. As for orders, the only way you find you can give her any instructions at all is to leave hopeful little notes on the sideboard, which all seem to have a vague aura of apology.

Not that she *minds*. She does everything she's asked. And often a bit more. There *was* that day when she tidied your make-up — and you came home to find all the disgusting little stubs and blobs and half-used tubes clean and orderly — and had to go out and re-stock everything out of shame.

Of course, it is lovely to come home to a clean, tidy house, smelling of disinfectant and loo cleaner and bleach ... and your Dior perfume??! But she *has* left a note suggesting the vet look at the cat's left ear. And she has repotted the African Violets. And she's put the remains of your currant cake out for the birds. And she's forgotten her carrier bag, with her library books.

Oh God. Not Freud. Jung.

Vacuum Cleaners

Plough, shear, shred, puff, spit, spark, shudder.
Leave tracks
Reject pins, tacks, bird-sand, cat-litter, thread, wool, lint, hair,
cactus, compost, talc and fluff.
Move dirt to other areas of carpet.
Swallow marbles, lego, hairpins, small silver, handkerchiefs,
  valances,
curtains, scarves, belts and shoe laces.
Go into convulsions.
Unravel carpets.
Veer, skitter, rush, stall.
Take chunks out of door posts and skirting boards.
Turn over on their backs.
Spring open.
Spew things previously devoured.
Refuse to rewind flex having the slightest kink, twist or curve.
Object to standard points.
Switch themselves off in mid career.
Switch themselves on again.
Roar, rattle, whine, hum, hiccup and vibrate.
Fight off any change of tool
or length of additional tubing.
Fall down stairs.
Electrocute charladies.

Treasures

Mrs Green ignored the loo
but shone the tiles like glass,
while Mrs Smith neglected drains
to concentrate on brass.
Hoovering through had no appeal
for Mrs Mary Stout,
but cupboards yielded up their dead
when she had turned them out.
The ironing was impeccable
in the hands of Mrs Clay,
but the level of the brandy sank
with every passing day.
.. They came, they went and some were good
and some were catastrophic.
Sometimes they smelled of my Chanel
and sometimes of carbolic.
At last, at last, a Treasure rose,
a sun to banish gloom.
She stripped the cooker to the floor
and spring-cleaned every room,
shampooed the rugs, de-flea'd the cat,
repaired the broken Ming,
polished the silver, mended shirts
and taught the birds to sing.
Flowers bedecked the drawing room,
even the apples shone;
the windows glittered like the dew
- then, suddenly, she'd gone.
And with her went the diamond brooch,
the green jade figurines,
the Georgian teaspoons and the pair
of silver soup tureens.

Our present lady, Mrs Brown,
is kind but ineffective.
Still, her one weakness seems to be
the Chocolate Digestive.

Em Comes to Work

"Mum! My child minder's given up! Mum, I'm desperate. Could
you ..."

"You *know* I can't, love ..."

"Just today ..."

"That's what you said when she had flu, dear — Em's a love, but I
can't take her to work with me. She's not naughty — she just
always gets under your feet."

"Just *once,* mum — the boss is short-staffed and I just can't let
him down at such short notice. She did go off to sleep last time
... maybe ..."

"Oh — all right, then. Once. Pop her round quickly or I'll be
late."

. . . .

"*Now,* Em. You've got to be very, very, very good. Promise?"

"P'omise. Toys?"

"No, no toys this time. It took me half an hour to pick up the last
lot. No, back to Auntie Gillie's. Where you had that nice sleep in
the little bedroom. *You* know Auntie Gillie. Auntie Gillie and
Uncle Peter."

"Nanny, come wif me see cat."

"I'm ironing, dear."

"Me iron."

"No, dear — not till you're a big girl."

"Nanny, sit down wif me. Let's *talk.*"

"Can't sit down, love; when I've done this I've got to hoover."

"Me help Nanny."

"No, love. You sit and look at the book ... Wouldn't you like to
go night-night? Like you did last time? In the pretty little bed?"

"Yus. Me toired. Me an' Tetti go ni' ni'."

" — Off you go to the loo then — and I'll put a dustbin bag under
the sheet, just in case. Though you never wet now, do you?"

"Nefer wet bed now. Big gel."

"This is auntie's Spare Room. Now, you're not to touch
anything. Nothing. Understand? You cuddle down with Tetti
and go to sleep and when you wake up, you can have a drink and
a biscuit and we'll go home."

"P'omise, nanny. Not touch nuthin. Good girl. Never touch

nuthin."

"There's my lamb. Nanny tuck you in. Now. I'll sit here just for a minute and then I must go down the stairs. I won't be far and Tetti can look after you while I'm gone. All right?"

"Alright, Nanny. Luf you. Tuck in."

(1½ hours later)

"Nanny! Come see! What dis?"

Nanny plods up the stairs. "There's a good girl, Emmy. Nanny's coming."

Enters bedroom: "OH MY GOD. Em! You are the WORST CHILD IN THE WORLD. You told me you wouldn't touch *any*thing. (Smack) Not *any*thing. (Smack) *Look* what you've done to auntie's room! Your friend Gillie! *Look* what you've done! (Smack) *How* am I ever going to get this cleared up?"

"Get into the bathroom. Stand still. Don't you *dare*. I don't *care* if there's soap in your eyes. Now. In here. SIT ABSOLUTELY STILL OR I WILL *KILL* YOU."

The bedroom had pale lilac walls, a pale pink, rose-scattered nylon coverlet, padded and frilled, on the single bed. The dressing table held make up, a wicker basket full of hair slides and oddments, bottles of Chanel No 5 and Arpège. in their original boxes. This no longer obtains. The walls are decorated with bold, sweeping designs, executed in red brick by Yardley. Nearest to the pillow an attempt has been made at a more intricate variation. The bravura of this work is echoed in heavier forms among the conventional roses of the quilt. A feeling of excitement has been brought to the overall concept by a scattering of half-sucked cough sweets, a dramatic spiked construction of hairgrips and curlers and by strong, blocked motifs on scent boxes, which have been transformed by a firm, textured layer of the same brick red. The denouement is, however, undoubtedly the heap of shoes piled on the bed with a brilliant suggestion of underlying chaos and liberally decorated in the same pigment.

The whole concept stuns and bewilders, affronts the eye and forces upon us the realisation ...

. . . .

Half an hour later the walls — mercifully painted paper — hold only a faint sunset glow in the corners of some of the raised motifs. Though a little of the original paper seems to be showing through in patches of khaki shadow.

The scent bottles stand naked on the dressing table, along with diminished sachets of cough sweets, small heaps of hair pins and the lipsticks Em hadn't got round to yet.

Miraculously, the shoes have cleaned up with never a stain. This cannot be said of the bedspread. The room has the look of someone who has just passed through a severe illness, a little worn and not quite itself.

Nanny is very tired. She is not quite herself either. Em is sitting exactly where she was thumped down. She is not at all sure whether or not she is allowed to move her eyeballs.

"*Get* into the pushchair. I've written the lady a note and we'll just have to hope that wall dries out well. Arms in your coat. You just *wait* till I see your mum. I've had about *enough*. And you sucked sweeties. *How* often have you been told never, never, never to eat *any*thing unless you asked Mummy or Nanny first? How many times? Do you know you could have made yourself very, very ill, Em? What happens to little girls who eat things they shouldn't eat?"

"Dey *doi*. Nefer see dere mummys no more. *Hever*."

"That's right. So you were extra bad. Now. We're going home. Sit still.

Don't you *dare* kick."

They take the hill at speed, fuelled by adrenalin and locked in their own black cumulus. Once the coverlet has been dumped violently on the counter at the cleaners, Em brightens. The evidence has obviously been got rid of. She starts to sing quietly under her breath. They pass the station.

"*Look,* Nanny. All de poopils gettin' off de trayin.'"

"Don't talk to me, Em. I am not yet in the mood."

Em curls into a ball of despair and escapes into sleep.

Her dad arrives to fetch her. He thinks it funny. Nanny's eyes narrow to slits. She kisses Em goodbye, but it lacks any real enthusiasm. She's thinking of Auntie reading that note. She's thinking of Auntie confronted by what was the newly-decorated spare room. She is thinking of her job.

The next evening Em turns up again. Her mum reports that she had to be persuaded to come as 'Nanny says neffer neffer neffer ave me at 'er 'ouse agin.' She sidles in. Nanny opens her arms and Em hurtles into them. There is a muffled conversation, mostly

consisting of Sowwys and Neffer Neffer Neffers.
Her mum says she will pay for the damage — and that Em has
already been taken to buy a replacement lipstick with the money
she was saving for a lion she coveted.
Nanny says O.K. — but it's the Last Time she ever looks after Em
in the day time.
"Oh, I'm giving up day work, anyway. Mum? Could you just look
after her for half an hour this evening?"
"*Now?*"
"Only half an hour."
"But ..."
"Won't be long, Mum."
"Din mean tread on your toe nanny."
"That's all right, love."
"Kiss it better. There. Now we haf a story, Nanny ..."

Mrs H and Me

Mrs Kay is fussy over mirrors.
Mrs Lee doesn't trust me with her plates.
Mrs Bridges goes to pieces
if her sheets have any creases
- but Mrs H and me - we're mates.

For I do the drains while she is washing nappies
and I do the rooms while she is at the shops.
The she gets young Tom to settle
and I puts on the kettle
and whatever we were doing - well, we stops.

She asks me what to do about the colic
and I tells her, having seven of me own
and we talk of Men and prices
and the international crisis
- for there's nothing like a biscuit and a moan.

So . . I never touch the ruddy flowered china
and I does the glass with Windolene and spit
but . . for Mrs H. I bake
me exclusive chocolate cake
and I've told old Mrs Bridges that I quit.

Mrs Blane

Mrs Blane was a kind, ordinary, decent woman who had made one catastrophic mistake in her ordinary, decent life. She had married a crook. Not a spectacular criminal able to keep her in unaccustomed splendour, but a man to whom it simply never occurred that there was another, far simpler and far more financially rewarding way of life to be had in doing a common-or-garden job of work. He did little deals, he helped out friends, he hovered round the back of lorries waiting for things to fall into his hands. Metaphorically. He was rarely involved in anything directly. He was a dogsbody. A stander on touch lines. I always knew when something had Come Up. No one in their right mind could fail to: it seemed incredible that the police ever missed the phenomenon. There was, for instance, the time that I came back from a short holiday to find the entire house transformed. It was like wading into a rain forest. Somewhere along the Great North Road a number of bales of blinding green material, slashed by a design of indigo lianas, had changed ownership. I couldn't but feel someone had shown a quite incredible incompetence, unless the manufacturers, wakening from their fit of lunacy, had done a deal in order to recoup from their insurance. Mr Blane, at any rate, seemed to have been unable to shift his share in the enterprise, and to have been forced to make the best use he could of it. Nearly every window of the house was curtained, most of them to the floor. Beds, chairs, alcoves, all lost in an impenetrable forest. Marooned in the crimson carpeted glade before the television (carpet and TV being products of former forays), Mrs Blane, exhausted by her efforts at the sewing machine, knitted to the rattle of Korean gunfire. Mr Blane, having relieved himself of his intolerable burden, had once again taken to the road.

I was there because Mrs Blane was dying — untidily, absent-mindedly, but certainly. She had continued her fight with the housework and her amiable, crooked kids for as many years as she could but as her strength failed, she had been obliged to call in the cavalry, which was me. A seasoned campaigner with a mop.

Cleaning the house was interesting, as researching a remote, disintegrating tribe would be interesting. I had never known, for one thing, that it was possible to fry an egg in deep fat. Or that cheese was still considered edible when it had attained the consistency of cracked marble. The tall, bony, smiling boys drifted through the house, abandoning cracked mugs with their sludge of cold tea and cigarette stubs, plates smeared with the congealed remains of their erratic meals, oily rags and money. There were little teetering piles of money throughout the house, on every ledge and shelf and table, small puddles of silver in every ornamental bowl, grubby notes under every clock.

When I first arrived the boys had been taking care of Mum as best they could, keeping up the fire, taking the wash to the launderette, knocking together what they considered tasty little meals to keep her strength up. The gas stove was a slow cascade of fat, the walls about it spattered, the floor a slithering danger. Saucers of lard stood about as back-up. The fridge was rich with bacon, pork and sausages, mould and wedges of ice.

I found a bucket, removed the sections of motor bike from it and brewed a concoction that devoured the fat and a little of the lino. The boys came in and watched. "Lovely that is. You're doing a good job there, Mrs Brown. Coming up a treat the stove is." I waited till their backs were turned before I packaged the opalescent fur-edged bacon and stuffed it to the bottom of the dustbin. There seemed to be a quite abnormal amount of it: one suspected it had been "acquired in bulk". The sausages were sealed and the expiry date permissible. I left them. The pork strips followed the bacon. There was no way of checking the eggs.

So. We had a kitchen. So heavy with the smell of bleach that it caught one's breath, but fat-free and uncluttered. The sparrows were fighting over the sweating cheese and the mould-flecked loaf. I trapped the youngest boy in passing and sent him to the shops for some fresh food, a few green apples. "But I aint' got no money!" I pressed the nearest leaning tower of silver into his hand. "And me bike's stripped down." I walked him to the door. The shops were a ten minute slouch away and the day was fine. The other two seemed a little stunned and retired to their bedrooms. They were not to remain undisturbed for long.

It was a house crammed with acquisitions — legitimate and otherwise. One stepped warily, opened cupboards carefully. The recurring question was, "Do you *really* need this Wayne?" Or Gary. Or Dave. As I got to know them better it changed: "You

don't need this, Wayne?" or Gary, or Dave. And they helped me
carry the cardboard boxes out to the yard. I tried to work it that
it all went out on bin day, knowing that if I didn't they would
have second thoughts, and rescue half their battered treasure. I
had a son myself.
Their rooms remained their own comfortable rat holes, heaped
about with records and magazines, playing cards and
paperbacks, sections of car and fragments of motor bike. But the
sheets on the beds were now clean and the clothes were in the
cupboards … I did not investigate the cupboards.
The loo was immaculate. Over the loo Mrs Blane still held sway,

and the boys knew it. China and plastic shone: it would have put to shame the diabolical lavatories of some of my more privileged employers.

They loved her. They gave her pies and processed peas, chips and eggs and tea with condensed milk. They never thought of flowers. She would have been astonished if they had. But they brought her in "Chinese" or cod and a double portion. And the racing papers. And fags.

And she loved them. Her good-hearted boys; who were always pressing one to a nice lighter, a nicer little watch, or a pair of classy jeans, which looked most wonderfully like the ones featured on 'Police Five'.

Mrs Blane sat on, carried to her armchair in the mornings. She was certain that the sickness was cheating in some way. She told me it was all a matter of will power; that she'd had a friend with the same thing who had just given in. Made no fight of it at all. And went into a home. Others she'd heard of, were almost normal year after year.

She made out her order list for the grocer. Got Dave to prune the roses … with dire results. Got him to send for catalogues. Although a wheelchair would have given her access to the summer world outside, she fought it off, and was lifted between bed and bathroom; marooned before the television.

She went on knitting, though I noticed as the months went by that it didn't seem to be getting anywhere in particular. Her face changed very little and her great mass of beautiful dark hair shone as if it had an entirely separate existence. A lady came to do it.

"My goodness, you've lovely hair. Not a touch of grey and so *thick*."

Mrs Blane accepted the compliment. Whatever else she lacked, she had magnificent hair, hair to envy. Even though the rest of her seemed to be blurring, growing cumbrous and unmanageable.

I hoovered about her, contesting the racket of the US cavalry or the drone of political debate. It was all grist to Mrs Blane, a window on the world that must be presumed to exist still, beyond the door. She sat in the garden less and less now. The novelty had worn off for the boys, and for her the bumping and the glare of sunlight had come to outweigh the adventure. I gathered snippets of local news, bringing them to her like

34

worms to a fledgling; supplied her with *Vogue* and *Country Life*
and the *Sunday Times Supplement,* garnered from other
employers.

When the boys were out on their legitimate or nefarious
concerns, we'd have a cup of tea, and she would tell me about
Him. Without apparent rancour, more as one would recount the
plot of a somewhat depressing novel. Though sometimes, when
the indignities and pains of her illness had become too much for
even her to bear, she would cry. Very quietly, holding her hands
tightly together. There was nothing one could do or say, but to
stroke the thick waving dark hair and hush her as one would a
child roused from nightmare.

But we got through the autumn and the winter and when spring
came she said she felt a lot better now that the days were
getting warmer. Sometimes the lads would wrap her up and
move the chair out into the garden, where the coltsfoot and
celandines shone among the remains of Dave's old Anglia and
the cat drowsed on a disintegrating mattress. Mr. B brought her
home a crate of Guinness that time. Said he would soon see her
right. But it didn't. She was taken very queer on the Saturday.
Pneumonia, Dean told me, and they came and took her away. She
never had got round to having a glass of stout. Mr B made a
horrible fuss at the hospital. Cried and cried and said she
couldn't die.

But she did.

Mrs Tiggywinkle Rides Again

The Laura Ashley housewife has flowered paper, in mud and
*   porridge,*
stripped pine or mahogany veneer, and brass at every turn
on stair
and lamp
and pot,
houseplants that drip from every surface, and never flower,
chipped plates armouring the walls,
alongside reproduction sepia photographs of unknown ancestors
and heavy-framed Millais.

Bygones everywhere.
Flat irons and wood-wormed spindles,
advertisements in tin for Stephens ink.
God help the char,
flung back a hundred years to deal and tile and bulbous, figured
glass,
and, best of all,
the ironing.
Frill, double frill and flounce,
pleat, double pleat and gathering,
tuck and ruche and inset lace,
drawn thread work,
piping.
And always linen, cotton, silk,
tumble-dried to corrugations.
Nightdresses to the floor and stiff as boards.
Buttons.
Petticoats.
Coverlets and tablecloths weighed down with crochet.
Bows.

Couldn't you fake a little, Ma'm?
A touch of polyester in the cotton sheets?
God knows your Automatic grinds away
behind the panelling
and Sainsburys have stocked your freezer.
The crock harbours Mother's Pride
alongside Marks and Spencers wholemeal.

(Those jars of pulses make a pretty show, but never lessen
and there's a film of dust on all the bunches of traditional herbs.)
The Teasmaid lurks on the bamboo table
beside the Pills and Librium.
The bookshelves house not Trollope or the Brontës
but Harold Robbins.
The oil lamp burns by wire.
The pianola's silent - music comes in three dimensions.

Come, Mrs H,
The Tiffany lamp is Tesco.
Compromise is all
What other century ever lived backwards?

Still - you supply a steam iron and an aerosol.
How do you see me?
A stand-in for all the ghostly maids?
A Mrs Tiggywinkle?
"An excellent clear-starcher"
I feel the shadow of a cap and apron wrapping me round.

I need the money, Ma'm
but
this afternoon, thank heavens,
I do the Jones,
Who are into High Tech.

37

Pet Hates

Stairs

All stairs. Carved. Suspended. Bare. Carpetted. Spiral. Loft. The lot. Stand the cleaner at the bottom and the nozzle will stretch just so far. Take it with you and it will suddenly plummet to the bottom. Take it to the top and it will threaten you like an avalanche. No cleaner invented, however, can really touch stair carpet. Especially in houses harbouring cats, dogs or incontinent flopsie bunnies. Ghosts appear on staircases, held back from eternity by the curses of generations of housemaids and dailies fighting hair, fluff, dust and stair rods.

Lego

Every char wishes the directors of Lego bankrupt and dishonoured.

Loos

Unflushed. Missed. Backed by python-like piping. Cradled in questionable carpet. Eccentric to flush. Perpetually without toilet rolls. Occasionally enlivened with Lego.

Windows
All windows. Wash, polish, rub to glittering perfection from
inside. Go outside and check. Smears. Mentally mark the
position and return indoors. They are invisible. Polish the
suspect area. You haven't touched them. Wrong window?
Wrong room? Wrong house?
The rich stay rich by the non-employment of professional
window cleaners.

Drains
"*Clever* Mrs Brown — I *know* you'll be able to track down
what's wrong. I've left a length of old curtain wire in the shed.
Paul says it's infallible."

Last Night's Washing Up
Unscraped, unrinsed. Left as a gesture in four inches of cold
water, rich with gobbets of fat and deposits of nameless sludge.

The Oven/Grill Pan
Kippers. Ugh.

Underbeds
Where kids keep most of their toys and cats disembowel rabbits,
where dogs are sick and adults leave tipped up glasses of gin,
cigarette stubs and underwear.

Outlet pipes
Full of hair. And gunk.

Kids
Who abandon half-eaten sticky things and roller skates on stairs.

Carpets
Deep pile, that harbour nuts, bolts, lipsticks, rubbers, elastic
bands … Sculptured, that protect dust and threads against all
assault … Cheap, that unravel … Cheaper, that moult … Velvety,
that show every movement, and the track of every cleaner.

Madam's Story

Key in the lock. Briefcase comes in first, followed by executive female, tired.

"She's been: well, thank God for that. You never know how long she'll spin out flu. Three weeks last time. Heaven knows, I only ask two mornings a week.

"She's really given the hall a thorough going over. Look at that parquet. She *loves* that polisher. I've seen her — ecstatic. Swinging the thing. High point of her day.

"God Almighty, she's been polishing. Why does she have to polish *every*thing. And it's that damned stuff she brings in with her. Bouquet de something. God, it makes one's nose itch ... I'll just have to leave her a note about it and damn the consequences. Makes the place smell like a brothel."

She droops into the living room.

"Well, at least she hasn't polished the teak. Lovely gloss she'd got on it before light dawned. No intelligence ... a kind woman, but no intelligence.

"She's been at the china cabinet. Surely ... no, she hasn't touched the Dresden. Well, she wouldn't — not after last time. Still, it must have shaken her when the glue dissolved. That poor little shepherdess lying there on the table with her legs on the ash tray.

"If she's touched that crossword. No, she's left it ... Wait a minute. I never did get 5 down — the sneaky bitch: she's faked my capitals. I'll *kill* that woman.

"Hoovered *under* the couch this time, I see. That's more like it ... God it's heavy. It'll just have to stay there till Julian gets back.

"She's left the Hoover out. A note: 'It's blowing rather than sucking again.' I don't know what's the matter with that woman. All right, so it's old. But there's *nothing* wrong with it. Can't be bothered to really strip it down, that's her trouble.

"She's left the stove. She has. She hasn't *touched* that grill. Look at it. An inch of fat *untouched*. What do I *pay* her for?

"And she's found the Bourbons. I left the Rich Tea where she could see them, but she had to root round for the Bourbons.

"She's done the ironing. That much at least. God, was there that much? The windows. Yes. And the paintwork. But she hasn't touched that mat. Still *full* of rabbit food. And there are still some droppings under the sideboard — she ought to get *under* it."

Trails upstairs.

"Bathroom smells nice. Bath positively *glittering*. Tiles a bit misty but ... that *bitch,* she's left a great wodge of hair in the outlet. She must have swilled the bath out, so she must have cleared the drain. I do believe she put it *back*. Oh it's time she went. But would I get anything better? They are *none* of them thorough nowadays.

"And that loo could be cleaner. Another note: 'Please tell children to flush the loo.' Now that's sheer impudence. She *knows* they are away, with Aunt Bea. Still, what can one say?

"She's just left Billy's room. Ankle deep in Lego. Oh, it's *too* bad. *And* she's left those hairpins just where I dropped the box this morning. *Dozens* of them. Absolutely no thought. *No* thoroughness."

Sniffs.

"She's been at my Miss Dior. One just can't *trust* these women. And look, she's stuffed all the loose change into the jar with those fivers — I'll have to rake it all out again. It's too bad.

"Jamaica was nice. She didn't seem a scrap interested. And I don't think she even *liked* that shell pendant. You'd think she'd adore something a bit exotic, out of her rut. God knows she could do with a little of the exotic. She's such a dowd. And I notice she never wears that blouse I gave her. Mother used to look marvellous in it.

"Ye Gods — *another* 'note', on the pillow. 'The Milkman says there is £24.50 to pay. Your husband phoned — says he'll be in late and you're not to wait up. The fish in the fridge is off. You need more scourer. The kitchen waste pipe is blocked again. Looks like food fragments. Suggest wire and/or Clearway. Thanks for chicken carcass and the colour supplements. Forgive 5 down — couldn't resist it! We have been accepted for Australia and will be sailing in a month. Lots to arrange, so I'm afraid this will be my last week. Will pop in Friday for a final dust round and leave key in larder. Best wishes.'

"The ungrateful *bitch*."

Don't you worry, Mrs A
— she'll be no trouble at all

42

Little Brat

"I go to school now."

"Yes, I know. Why aren't you there today? Is it a holiday?"

"No. I felt ill. I felt all ill and hot and prickly and sick and Mummy said I was to stay home."

"You look all right now. Do you feel better?"

"No. I feel *terrible*."

"I wouldn't go eating that sticky chocolate then, love."

"Like it. My daddy has a very big car."

"Yes, I've seen it. A *lovely* car."

"You haven't got a car."

"No. No car. I don't really need one."

"Everyone needs a car."

"Not me."

"Then you're silly."

"I certainly am."

"I got a new dress for dressing up. Mummy got it for me."

"Very pretty indeed. Was it for a birthday?"

"No. I wanted it. I saw it and I wanted it."

"Lucky old you."

"She's going to get me another one. A pussy cat one. With a tail. I'm going to wear it for Joanne's party. Joanne has a swimming pool. And two ponies."

"Lucky old Joanne. Bet she'll like your cat dress."

"She'll be ever so jealous. Mrs. Brown. You haven't cleaned the kitchen floor for ages."

"Yes I have dear. Just this minute. Get off it. Please."

"This is my mummy's kitchen."

"Yes, I know it's your mummy's kitchen, dear. But I'm cleaning it and when I'm cleaning it, I'm in charge. Run along, there's a good girl."

"No."

"All right then, stand there."

(Goes to living room to Hoover. Picks up coins.)

"Why are you picking those up, Mrs Brown?"

"Look, I'll put them on the side. I think they are out of your little handbag. Be careful to pick things up or they'll end up in the Hoover."

"Doesn't matter. Daddy will give me some more."

"That's not the point ... How's your cat?"
"Not a cat. It's a kitten."
"It's two years old and the size of a terrier, love. It's a cat."
"Kitten."
"Ah well. Just move that pram, will you dear?"
"No."
"Here we go, then."
"You mustn't move my pram!"
"If I'm to hoover this room, I move the pram.
"Mummy, she moved my pram!!"
"Oh, I'm sure Mrs Brown didn't *mean* to move it. Were you
playing with it, dear?"
"Yes, I was playing with it. And *she* moved it."
"I'm sure Mrs Brown will get it for you — you mustn't cry, my
lovely one. Mrs Brown? Mrs *Brown?* ... I think Mrs Brown's gone
home. She must be feeling tired. Never mind, you can have the
house all to yourself, dear. Can mummy fetch you a piece of
cake?"

Give an Inch

Pick up two teddy bears.
A month later you'll be picking up six colouring books, forty-seven crayons, three trodden on chalks, three bears, one doll, one snoopy, five bead necklaces, one spilled bag of jellies, the contents of the dolls house, one half-eaten mars bar, four broken biscuits, a spilled water jar, three paint-loaded brushes, a wet paint box, fifteen sheets of tracing paper and a ground-in collection of cockle shells.
Don't *start*.

Time to Leave

You know that you have finally been accepted by the household when they give up having a quick tidy up before you come, when the bath is left with a dense grey rim of scum, when the kitchen sink is blocked with cooled cabbage, when someone has tied all the dining room chairs together with string, when there is a drift of dirty socks under the bed, when there is a frozen niagara of fat down the side of the stove, when all the pots have been left to soak, when every lid and cap in the kitchen, bathroom and bedroom has been left off and there are little puddles of toothpaste, face cream and glue on every surface.
This is the time to leave.

Mrs Ramsbottom's Revenge

"Angela? Oh. Angela, dear. It's Mrs Ramsbottom. No, not me, dear. This is Frances, dear. *My* Mrs Ramsbottom. The Treasure. Yes, the one who polishes *under* the sideboard. Mmm. The one who relines all the drawers. That's her. She's gone mad. No, she's not in the asylum. She's here. My dear, I don't know what to do. She was just the same as usual. Came bristling in at nine, put on her pinny and got stuck into the breakfast things.

"I don't know what triggered it. But it may have been the egg. Yes, the egg. It was off. Very green. Peter just let out a *vile* expletive and left it. And I couldn't bear to touch it. So there it was.

"She made a funy sort of *gagging* noise when she wrapped it up and put it in the bin. But after all, it's her *job*. You don't get a dog and bark, now, do you?

"I thought she was over it, but you know how these things always come together. Yes, Trixie. Yes, she'd been sick *again*. Right in the middle of the living room. And she trod in it. No, not Trixie. Mrs Ramsbottom. She went pale. My dear. *Chalk* white. Of course, she mopped it up. She always *does* mop it up, doesn't she? Never said a *word* before.

"Well, I thought she was back to normal. Didn't say much. I was doing the flowers and she hoovered round me just as she usually does. Picked up all the fallen petals. Not a *word*.

"Finished off downstairs. Swept and dusted and polished and did all the glass and trotted up the stairs with the cleaner. Merry as a wedding bell, one would have said. And then she let out a sort of high pitched whistling noise. I just *flew* up. I thought she'd electrocuted herself. You *know* that vacuum cleaner. Oh, it's perfectly serviceable. But it does *spark* a bit. And there she was, staring into the bath. Well, it was a bit yukky. It's that new bath oil. Marvellously effective, but it leaves a sort of *scum* all round the bath ... all round the bath ... oh, you know. And then there was the henna. And there did seem rather more hair in the waste pipe than usual. My hair seems to absolutely *fall* out since that last perm. It's Antoine you know. He is nowhere as good as Pierre. I've said it before. . .

"Oh, Mrs Ramsbottom? Well, as I said, she was just standing there, *puce*. My dear, *puce*. And suddenly she just grabbed the

loo cleaner, the *loo* cleaner, my dear, and she just squirted it all
over the bath. And all up the walls. And then she tipped an entire
drum of scourer down the loo. God alone knows what she's
done to the enamel. My dear — dark green, as you know. It will
show every mark.

"I just *fled*. I mean, I *yelled* at her, but she didn't seem to hear.
She seems to be in the master bedroom now. With the pink glass
cleaning stuff. And a bottle of ammonia. My Chinese carpet! My
God, what *am* I to do? The police? Yes, I suppose I should. It's
just so *unreal*.

"Mrs Ramsbottom — I mean, she's the salt of the earth. I pay her
far less than I did that awful Mrs Robertson and she does *twice*
as much. And babysits at a moment's notice …

My God, Angela. She's coming down the stairs. What *is* she doing
with that loo brush? Oh *no,* Mrs Ramsbottom! *Please* Mrs
Ramsbottom! Aaggh!!"

"Mrs Cley-Abbott? Mrs Warburton-Brown is indisposed, I'm
afraid. I wonder if you'd be so good as to call back later."

Beware of the Char

Never cross your char. She might starch your underpants.

A cleaner is someone who can reduce an antelope rug to the appearance of a savaged goat.

A long established char becomes a sort of relation. And we all know about relations.

Never try to upstage your char. She knows to ten pence how much a week you spend on groceries. And how much on booze.

If anyone refers to me as a Mrs Mop I will bite him in the thigh.

When your char leaves a bald mop in a bucket in the middle of your kitchen, it's time either to apologise or get another char.

Three bits of Lego and your char will mutter 'Boys'. A couple of hundred, and you'd better write out another postcard for the tobacconist's.

The lady novelist who tells the press, with a brave smile, how she copes alone with a career and four children has just heard the back door close behind the Daily.

Children who feel themselves superior to your char may be instrumental in your finding yourself without one.

Beware the suddenly ecstatic char. She's either come into money, getting remarried, or has decided to give in her notice anyway.

Every char has her breaking point. For some it is dog shit on the living room carpet. For others it's that the biscuit tin is always empty.

48

Madam!

A cleaner is someone who speaks of you to her friends with kindness — but as one speaks of a backward child.

A char judges you by your loo , not your academic qualifications.

With the smallest twist of fate, Madam, you could be in my shoes. So don't come it ...

Remember — Madam Today, Char Tomorrow

Never ask your char why she is leaving you, yet continuing to do for a woman who pays less and lives further.

You know you've gone too far when the char swills out the bath — and then replaces the plug of hair in the outlet.

"I asked if I could have her *Times* when she'd finished with it — she was *so* pleased, bless her. Hadn't the heart to tell her they are for putting under the new carpet."

Your children may be paragons in your eyes. To your char they are the little buggers who never flush the loo.

Ladies don't really like their chars to hum Don Giovanni.

The thing best calculated to madden a char is the lady of the house drifting from room to room moaning gently that she has *so* much to do today —while the char works flat out around her.

It's not so bad cleaning for someone who is rushed off her feet in a job, or who is ill, but women who just can't be bothered get put down for extermination when the revolution comes.

Speak nicely to your char — she's probably booked the lamppost she's going to hang you from.

49

Favourite Things

Charring gives you access to other people's heat, light, coffee, radio, daily paper, telephone and lavatory roll. And biscuit tin. And they pay you for it!

Cleaning houses is better than standing in a dole queue. It's warmer, and there's a biscuit tin.

In Heaven I shall hear the cry, "Tea Up, Mrs Brown!"

Every char has her favourite note. One of the most popular is "Leave the hoovering today and .."

Being a char is rather like having the run of a film set.

Charring after all offers variety — you can clean the loo *before* you do the beds, or afterwards. Big deal.

Almost every unskilled job entails day-long chatter ... if you're a char you can choose whether to speak to the budgerigar or not.

In what other job can you continue to follow 'The Sullivans'?

In charring you start out with employers and end up with friends.

Genes

Some women get their kicks
from polish, soap and water
and so instil
domestic skill
in each obedient daughter.

My mum washed down the lino
and mangled Monday through
but she thought, with guilt, and secretly,
there were better things to do -
and she propped up Dostoevsky
while she chopped the Irish Stew.
She taught me that a household
must rest upon routine.
But I didn't see the discipline -
I only saw the dream.

And Gran, at the shout of a Willesden thrush
would abandon her mop and pail and brush
and wheedle us out for a ride on the tram
and a nice little bit of fatty ham
and a cup of tea and a bun
"for you can't stay in on a day like this
- you just can't waste the sun."

And Great Grandma was diligent
unless she heard the call
of a paddle boat bound for Clacton
- when she let her duster fall.
And back and back through the centuries
the females of my line
did wonders with the housework
- if they could find the time.

At last the gods took notice
of my rollicking family tree
- and said "This really has to stop,"

- and stop it did, with me.
For they nodded over my cradle
"The whole thing's gone too far.
A Woman's Place Is In The Home,
We'll make this one a Char."

So despite my inclinations
I scrub and sweep all day
- but the gods forgot one simple fact,
It's housework done for pay.
So every loo pays off the Rates
and every drain the Heating.
With every swoosh of the balding mop
my milk bill takes a beating.
And when I clean an oven
Or Hoover down the stairs
I'm buying a longed-for paperback
or a couple of cream éclairs

And when I'm home in the evening
I happily confess
I sprawl in a chair and drink my tea
and ignore the surrounding mess
And I plan for a little coach trip
and a week beside the sea
as my ancestors grin and nod their heads
and scheme along with me.

My Friend Tim

Veronica had the face of an intelligent and Paris-bred weasel. She was married to Ben, who was virtually non-existent, though presumably having substance in Toronto, Rome, Hong Kong and Frankfurt, to which cities, among others, he was constantly being summoned at short notice. Evidence of his corporality rested on the material he left in his wake: sweaty shirts, incredibly brief underpants, bottles of perfume to add to those stacked in Veronica's bedside cupboard, dolls to supplement the untouched regiment in Samantha's room, lumps of exotic rock for Tim.

Veronica was a lecturer. Not a teacher. A lecturer. Sixth Form College. Doted on by her young male students, a selection of which came round at times to discuss Donne in depth and to read her their verse. An advocate of Freedom, Women's Liberation and an employer of me, the char, and Sabine, the Au Pair. Whom she terrified for her own good. She didn't terrify me and she knew and resented it in a restless, nervous way, prancing about me on her small, neat paws, wondering if there was anywhere she could plant her tiny sharp teeth. In the interim she decided to treat me as a Fellow Woman. This entailed leaving me the usual long list of jobs to complete with little heart-to-heart, equal-to-equal requests. Could I check Samantha's maths, hear Samantha's Vivaldi piece, see that Samantha ate her salad. Could I find out why Tim was in such a vile mood. Could I do *something* about Sabine's use of the past tense? Could I lend her my copy of 'Wives and Daughters' again? Could I come back on Thursday evening and check through her thesis with her. (Interesting to note that as char I got coffee and walked home, as thesis checker I got whisky and a lift.) Could I clean out the cupboard under the stairs and phone the gas company about the faint smell in the garage and the vet about the dog's snuffles. (To a man they disliked the dog. The fact that I passed the time of day when I came in stunned the creature. He would sit in whichever room I was cleaning hoping that I might just pat him again. I can only presume he was a Token Dog.) Could I repot the geranium?

I could. I did. The odd, tricky, puzzling bits are the only ones that make a char's life bearable.

Sabine cried on me. She spent a great deal of her spare time in her room. Sulking, said Veronica. Weeping, said Sabine. No effort, said Veronica. No friends, said Sabine. She had not time to make friends, unless one counted the nodding acquaintances as she walked the dog, which terrified her, twice a day. A small group of other au pairs, too, whom she met at her weekly English class — a rather mournful band. Veronica lent her clothes, fed her admirably — on the food she, Sabine, cooked of course — and scolded her. Usually in front of the children.

The children, especially Samantha, given this apparent seal of approval, scolded her too.

"Mrs Brown. You know, Sabine's so *silly*. Can't take any sort of joke. Talks on the phone for hours — in *French*. She's supposed to be over here learning English, not French. Whoever heard of a German coming to England to learn *French*."

After a while my stony face and my obvious liking for the solid, sad German prevented baiting while I was actually present, though heaven alone knows what she continued to endure while I was absent. My feeble lectures on 'Just imagine if *you* were away from home ...' sounded uninspired, even to me. The children, carving out an existence for themselves in the vacuum they inhabited, could scarcely see her as anything else but spineless. They had no route to empathy, no way of visualising the close family life she'd left behind in Salgau.

I loathed them. Sharp as their mother and too clever by half. Their bodies seemed too young to house those eyes.

Until I found a note from Veronica, 'Tim in bed with stomach upset. If he's hungry, eggs in fridge.'

Tim was reading 'Roy of the Rovers,' not the 'Nicholas Nickleby' on the bedside table. The sharpness had blurred out of him, he was snuffly, hot and thirsty. He did not want an egg, just something to drink. I suspected there was an interdict on soft drinks in the house, but, lacking written confirmation, went down to the local shop.

Staring at me over the bubbles he asked how long I would be in the house. "Couple of hours."

"Good. It's nice having someone to talk to." He slithered down the pillow a little.

"Like your aircraft.You make them?"

"Mm. That's my best. The Lancaster."

"Nice. Used to see those, you know, limping home after night raids. Went out in formation, came back in a straggle. Engines gone. Long gaps."

"You in the war then?"

"About your age."

"You're nearly as old as my gran then. Didn't know that. We don't see her often. She and Mum don't get on."

"Going to make more of these models?"

"Not worth it really. Mum doesn't like clutter. Says human beings should travel light. When I've got more than five she makes me get rid of them. I bury them in the wood."

"Bury them?"

"I don't like putting them in the bin. And Mum says burning plastic is pollution."

"Oh. Yes, I suppose it would be. Did your dad bring you back that crystal?"

"Yes. Brought it back from Brazil. He goes to Brazil quite a bit. Sam and I don't like it much, him going all over."

"Why's that? He brings you back some nice things ... and it's a good job."

"It's the aircraft. We always think he's going to crash one day. Mum says it's silly. But you read about it."

"Oh, I should think he's safe as houses. They say it's safer than crossing the road."

"That's what Mum says. But you see it in the papers. I'm going to go to boarding school next year. Did Mum say?"

"Half spoke of it."

"I thought I was going to St Benedicts. All my friends are."

"But the new school will be exciting, too, I expect."
"Mum says it's got a higher standard. That means they push you."
"But you are clever — you'll be all right."
"Oh, I know I'm clever. But I get panicky if someone starts pushing. I did before. I got ill."
"Ill?"
"Mum had to take me to a child psychologist. Said I was showing disturbed behaviour."
"Why on earth did she say that?"
"I think it was when I bit her that time."
"Well, I expect she knew something was wrong. Tell you what. I'll have a look around at home and see if I can find some Lancaster stamps. You can have them to help your British collection. Now then, tea ... And I'll see if I can find some biscuits."
"Mum leaves out Maries in the tin. But *I* know where she keeps the Garibaldis. In the TV drawer, in a blue box."
"Squashed fly biscuits. Oh, I love those!"
"Right! You get them. We'll have a sort of picnic!"

DEAR VERONICA I HAVE DECIDED THAT AFTER ALL, I WILL BE ABLE TO MANAGE THREE DAYS A WEEK. I WILL, THEREFORE, BE IN ON WEDNESDAY. I WILL COME IN IN THE AFTERNOONS AND WOULD BE GLAD TO HAVE TIM'S TEA READY FOR HIM WHEN HE GETS IN, IF THIS IS AGREEABLE.

"You found them! There's six! Three each! You can have the one with the extra squodge of currants."

. . . .

Tim moved and Sam. Sam, who it turned out wasn't that keen on Vivaldi. Not on the piano. She wanted to play the oboe, but Mum said it hadn't the scope.
Sabine gave me the recipe for her hazelnut cake, said a tearful goodbye to her fellow au pairs and went home, fatter, sadder, wiser. I don't know what happened to the dog.
Veronica got her PhD. Somewhere or other she's listening to acne-ridden young men reading her poems about wombs and darkness. I never did get back 'Wives and Daughters'.
I presume her husband is still keeping her topped up with perfume. She hates perfume.

Youth Disguised

Old Mr Simpkin lived in one of the Railway Cottages, built, presumably, when steam had at long last reached the town, to the accompaniment of the local brass band and a burst of bucolic cheering. But steam had long since departed, along with the dog carts, the platform flower beds and the shining brass buttons. The cottages were charming, red brick, damp and falling apart. The owners of the land wanted Mr Simpkin out, along with his equally ancient neighbours, so that they could dig up the privet, root out the orchard, level the gooseberries and build a fine new pub.

I was sent in by the Council to clean for Mr Simpkin, who couldn't get about as nimbly as he once did, being on the very edge of ninety. He hated being on the edge of it. The real Mr Simpkin looked out of a deeply framed sepia photograph on the wall — the Mr Simpkin who was now locked inside the old bones that the damp tweaked and tormented. A young man of eighteen, hair sleeked down from a centre parting, nervous of the camera, dressed in his church-going suit. With two wives and a couple of wars ahead of him but, for the moment, safe in a respectable job, doing up parcels in a London haberdashers, and sometimes permitted, if his hands were immaculate, to take a parcel to the carriage waiting at the kerb.

The whole house was meticulously neat, the wide brass bed under its white cotton coverlet in the unheated bedroom, the dark little living room with the stairs hidden in an apparent cupboard, the brick-floored ice box of a scullery with its stone sink, its brass cold water tap and its gas stove perched on little curved legs.

Officially I was to Clean But Not Polish. Apparently polishing was considered to be a wicked extravagance and a waste of local government time. I polished. There was, after all, very little to polish. The only really polishable object in the house was the knobbly, mirrored, ornament loaded sideboard, but that I brought to the glowing perfection Mr Simpkin desired.

"I'll leave you that, I will. Don't you let 'em 'ave it. That's *yourn*."

I made a bit of a mess of the passage from the scullery to the living room, putting my trust in patent cleansers and polishing the coal dust into rather than out of the lino. I was scolded and went back to the brush and suds.

We had a ritual, Mr Simpkin and I. When I'd done the scullery, sweeping up the fallen whitewash, giving the tap a last burnish, and had returned to the firelit living room, Mr Simpkin would pull himself up from his armchair, that had been dragged as close to the coals as was possible without going up in flames. "Can't get warm, dear. You feel my hands. It's no good: can't get any warmth to them."

He regarded me, char transformed to guest.

"Now, you'd like a cup of tea, wouldn't you? You sit yourself down." And I would sit in the gloom, under the innocent gaze of the younger Mr Simpkin, the glare of the china cat, the thin ticking of the fairground prize clock, and listen to the sound of slippers on brick, to the clatter of kettle, gush of water, small roar of gas. Back he would come.

"Chocolate biscuits this week. My daughter's been. Means well. Nice girl. Like her mother. She was my second, you know. A good woman. Meant well."

The second wife was a shadowy affair, poor woman. It was not of her Mr Simpkin dreamed in the cold, damp bed with only the china hot water bottle for companionship.

Sometimes he would talk of her, in a faraway voice — more to himself than me.

"I dreamed about her last night. It was so real I think she *must* have been here. Smiling away she was. Always smiling when she was alive, you know. We never had any children, but it didn't matter. Never thought she'd go before me ... I don't mind going, you know. Not a bit. I'll be back with her then, you see. I know she's waiting. Know it."

The kettle whistled and he went off to make the tea. I thought of his poor puffed, ice cold hands and waited nervously, but back he came with the pot. I had the flowered plate ready and the knitted cosy. He fetched the two blue and white cups to the table, the sugar, the milk jug. I was allowed to open the biscuit tin, too stiff for him. "Got no strength in me hands now, dear." When summer came he would go down the garden and pick me flowers. "Don't you tell 'em, girl. Not supposed to do no bending. Don't you let on."

The men from the property developers turned up at regular intervals. I always knew when they had been, for they left the old man shaky and anxious. The lure of alternative accommodation

having failed, his dear ghost out-valuing any offer of central
heating and an electric stove, they resorted to bullying.
"They want me out, want all of us out. And they don't care how
they do it. I couldn't manage nowhere else. Me daughter says
she'd take me, offered straight off. She's a good girl.
But where would *I* fit in, with the dog and the children and all the
rest of it? Never thought I'd end up a burden to no one. And I
manage very nicely, here. Suits me. And there's the garden."
And the crumbling outside loo, the rotting brickwork, the cracks
reaching further and further across the ceilings.
I grew almost afraid to lift the latch of the back door, to call "Cooee.
You there, Mr Simpkin?" To go into the living room with news of
the weather and any innocuous gossip I had mustered. More and
more often the armchair was empty, the grate cold.
"Thought I'd stay put today, dear. If you could bring me up a cup

60

of tea later on, it would be nice. Don't seem to be able to get warm today."

The swollen blue hands on the cotton coverlet. He seemed half lost in the wide bed, in the cold room. The two white busts of Victorian goddesses on the mantlepiece caught the morning light and seemed to freeze it as it touched them.

A cup of tea and his hot water bottle refilled.

"Shall I pop across and get you the newspaper?"

"No dear. Don't feel like reading much today. Feel a bit warmer now. Think I'll have a little doze."

I shone the empty rooms, went up to see if he was comfortable, said goodbye — and went out into the warm sunlight, leaving him in the cold, quiet upstairs room.

Sometimes, though, he was not only up, but at the bottom of the garden, among the raspberry canes.

"Lovely crop we'll have this year. Raspberries and cream with our tea. Just you wait."

The children came in with me to see him sometimes, to drop off a pot of jam or a magazine. He gave them biscuits and told them they were good children, and they worried about him. Once when we were going away for a week on holiday, he vanished up into the bedroom and returned with a ten shilling note, which he pressed into the eldest child's hand.

"You get yourself some sweeties, dear. You and your brother and sister."

She was very quiet going home and I suddenly realised she was crying.

"He *shouldn't* have. It's ever such a lot for him — he's only on a pension. Oh, he *shouldn't* have."

They got him in the end, of course. I will always wonder if it was that great glowing bunch of wallflowers he gathered for me which brought on the attack that betrayed him into their hands. His daughter came and took him away in the family car. I don't know whether she took the two white busts, or the clock, or the staring cat. I doubt it. At any rate, she did not have him long. He died before the dealers cleared the house. And three years before the owners pulled it down. That smart young man in the suede jacket need not have plagued him so.

They built their pub. I don't know whether Mr Simpkin haunts it. I doubt it, for he wasn't a drinking man, and he is, I hope, more happily occupied.

«"Fine Feathers..."»

Ironing bundled anyhow
and needles down the chairs.
Playdoh in the carpet
and scooters on the stairs.
No one flushes anything
and no one stops to think
to scrape the greens and gravy
from the dishes in the sink.
The bath is rimmed with oily grime,
the drain is choked with hair,
the towels lie sodden in a heap
and talc is everywhere.

Most elegant the lady,
Most intelligent her spouse.
I wish that they'd apply it
to the running of their house!

Who Dunnit

The curtain always rises
on the char.
No surprises.
She's there for light relief,
never proves to be the murderer,
much less the ace detective.
Grief
never attends her finding of the corpse.
Only a shriek,
in dialect.

But one day, Madam,
if you must persist
in blocking up the drains with hair
I'll change the billing.

... This char
will star.

62

'ello Luv

The image of the working class, heart-of-gold char, with
her curlers and scarf, her overall and cheery Cockney repartee,
her fag and her cup of Indian tea — as used by almost every ad
man pushing a new cleaning product, every writer of detective
stories, every hilarious sit. com. ideas man — is closely related to
the working class, heart-of-gold whore. Neither exists
outside the imagination of the literary hack.

. . . .

Sadly, a great many employers suffer from the Little Eva
syndrome, passionately believing in the single-minded devotion
and loyalty of their faithful, grateful Daily.
Alas, the days of the old retainer are long gone — if they ever
existed outside the imagination of middle class novelists with
upper class dreams.
The average flesh and blood char would drop you without one
second's hesitation, without regret or anxiety, if something
better came up. And she's quite likely to be cursing you in fluent
BBC English

You Were Just One More Madam

Dear Madam, how trusting you are. You have given me a key to your home, access to your jewellery case, the free run of your biscuit barrel. Gin, whisky, Rice Krispies and Chanel No 5 lie open before me. Your talc, your skin cream are mine for experiment. Your loo paper for my filching, your bookshelves for my browsing. And, oddly, you are correct in your judgement; but how did you know? Do I look honest? Or too dull to indulge in normal inquisitiveness and female experiment? Or is it simply that you need my services so desperately that you are prepared to take a leap in the dark? At least you don't mark the whisky label. I looked, out of curiosity. And I think all the loose change scattered through the house is sheer carelessness, not entrapment, as it was in Victorian days. Oh yes, Madam, I know my ancestry. Times have changed and I sleep at home in my own bed, not in your attic. I am easy on your conscience for you have told yourself that I am your equal. Though, if I found more interesting employment tomorrow, your feminist principles would be most horribly shaken. In fact, I think, from past experience, that you would be very angry indeed, and consider me a most ungrateful wretch.

I know a lot about you. I know, of course, the executive lady who sometimes gets home before I leave. I wonder what your colleagues would make of you then, sprawled in a chair, your shoes kicked off, your face worn down to the skin. I wonder what they would make of you in the throes of a heavy cold, crimson-nosed and disconsolate, whimpering for hot blackcurrant cordial. Or on the day they phoned from Ian's school?

I know your taste in music. I know the records you felt obliged to buy, and the ones you play. I know you drink a good deal too much sherry when Sir is away in Hong Kong or Rio or Rome. I know all about the elegant middle-aged doctor ... There's nothing in it. You appear extremely sophisticated, Madam, but you are old fashioned at heart — and a little afraid of consequences. And gossip.

Strangely, Madam, you seem quite helpless in domestic crises. A leaking washing machine or a spluttering gas jet deprive you of all sense and ability. Your world of work is as remote to me as my own domestic existence is to you, but I have heard you spoken of with vast respect as a maker of decisions, a chivvier of secretaries, at times, a terrifier of The Board. Yet the failure of the cistern has you clutching your head and staring at the Yellow Pages in an agony of indecision. Which is comforting.

You work far harder than me, Madam, solve more problems, shoulder more responsibility. You make something of what in other hands would have deteriorated into an absolute nothing. I know that I could not cope with any of it ... particularly Sir, and I would not under any circumstances change places with you.

So I will not swig your whisky. Save perhaps for half a glass at Christmas. I will ration myself to three biscuits with my coffee. I will iron your silk underwear very carefully, and clean the perfumed oil from your pale yellow bath. Your possessions are safe. In actual fact,I do not covet much that you have — cleaning it has reduced it to a series of problems in polishes and soap. I will do my best to earn my pay.

But in return, Madam, please do not tell me every glorious detail of your Bermudan holiday, much less bemoan its difficulties. Don't tell me how hard it is to get by on your income. And, please, do not leave pears to rot in the big ceramic bowl, or boxes of cheese to liquify on the kitchen windowsill.

I've worked for you for a year and a half now, and it's almost time to go, for I have grown very tired of the pattern of your carpet and the fact that the cleaner picks up practically nothing but pile. I'll give you plenty of time to find someone else.

No, I won't miss you, Madam. I really haven't seen a great deal of you, though, like all chars, I've pieced together more of your life than you'd believe. It's an occupational, compulsive thing. I can assure you all your small secrets are perfectly safe with me — even the whereabouts of your one good string of pearls. On the whole I am for you a shining, tidy house, a faint smell of disinfectant and furniture polish. You leave the money on the table and it vanishes.

I could have turned into Mrs Jones or Mrs Robinson in mid-career and I don't think you would have noticed. So long as the oven was clean.

It's not been an eventful relationship, Madam. We've left very little mark upon each other. Some I have been more fond of, some I have loathed.

You, at least, flushed the loo.

In Madam's Own Words

Missus to Mrs Mop

"My dear — when you *first* came I used to *scuttle* around before you arrived in the morning and tidy up!

"But you have been so *marvellous* I feel now I can leave it *all* to you. I just don't do *any*thing now — you know how to run everything so much better than me!"

("This one should be titled, 'How I Lost My Char' - PB.)

"Dear Mrs B, saw Tom about iron and hoover of which you complained. He tells me you are perfectly safe if you don't touch the bare wires. Will try to get them seen to some time next week."

"My dear, I've absolutely *no* change. Could you pop back on Monday?"

"Oh, could you change his nappy, Mrs B? My nails aren't dry."

"Dear Pam. Won't it be *lovely* for you while we're in Bermuda? You'll be able to get all the carpets up and really *attack* them, won't you? I've hired a lovely carpet shampooer for you.
And, oh yes, the sweep will be coming. On the Wednesday. Not your usual day, I know, but it's all he could offer.
"I know you don't mind. You *can* manage, *can't* you — you know, I absolutely *rely* on you ..."

Missus to friend

"I *loathe* Mondays — I have to get up at six to clear up before the char comes in."

"My dear — she's a jewel. Can't *wait* to get her hands on the really gungie jobs. I really think she *loves* drains."

"Celia. My Mrs Roper has gone and won the Pools. Isn't it a giggle.£75,000!! Went absolutely mad — shot off to Bermuda with her entire family. I *do* hope she remembers she must be back by the 17th. I've got Arthur's Boss and Mrs Boss coming to dinner ... I simply *cannot* cope without her handling the washing up ..."

66

"My God, it's my char!"

Commandments for Madam

Thou shalt not . . .

. . . tell your char you don't do a *thing* between her visits — aren't you naughty???

. . . bring the spaniels across the newly scrubbed floor — and then be *witty* about it.

. . . ask your char to a cocktail party for fun. (She may upstage you!)

. . . address your char with the kindly condescension you reserve for very small children and the blind. (Turn over the fact that *they* don't like it either)

. . . tell your char how your shoulders ache from carrying the shopping from the supermarket to the car — when you know darned well she carries hers home from the High Street. (Remember? You *waved* last time you passed her.)

. . . set the central heating, in icy weather, to switch on as she leaves.

. . . convince yourself the lower classes *like* cleaning drains.

. . . expect a middle-aged fat lady to go tippy toes along your ice smooth working surfaces to clean the tops of cupboards.

. . . expect your char to know all the specialist museum techniques for cleaning objets d'art — while supplying her with nothing but scourer and Jeyes Fluid.

. . . tell your sixteen-stone char the secrets of your diet — which is centred round fillet steak.

. . . install acres of mirror-doored wardrobes.

. . . forget to re-stock the biscuit tin.

. . . just step out of your clothes as you move — and leave them there.

. . . leave half-eaten fruit down the sides of chairs.

. . . leave roller skates on the stairs.

Thou shalt not use talc.

Thou shalt not leave the gas stove looking as if you'd fried a horse on it.

Commandments for Cleaners

Thou shalt not . . .

. . . scrub the oil paintings.

. . . give the porcelain a good going over with a nail brush.

. . . attack the new fibreglass bath with scourer.

. . . tidy the book case into matching colours and sizes.

. . . wash the thermal underwear in the boil wash.

. . . use her face flannel to clean the bath.

. . . dust with her knickers.

. . . drag the vacuum cleaner from room to room, cannoning it off door posts.

. . . empty the dustpan into the rubber tree pot.

. . . spend more than five minutes reading the bedside 'Perfumed Garden'.

70

. . . plonk her dried flower arrangements back, back to front, after you've had a go at getting all the grass seeds off.

. . . rearrange Madam's ornaments into straight lines every time you dust.

. . . use the phone to have a chat with your daughter in Aberdeen.

. . . *keep* telling your lady that your children make their beds every day. Once is enough

. . . query her quotations, or worse, correct them.

. . . eat her last sugar almond.

Advice to Other Chars

Never shake an animal skin rug. It is hard to disguise two halves of an antelope.

Always think twice before you wash your employer's best china. If you succumb, leave the pieces neatly together in one place.

Leave any unspeakable vessel to soak, preferably outside the back door. Eventually they will run out of vessels.

Never sew on a button out of kindness. Next week you'll get the darning.

When she says, "I like the beds out *every* day", try 'em. The last char probably left with a slipped disc.

Lay up for yourself qualifications in your youth — for then you will not be obliged to clean other people's lavatories in your old age.

Baby and Me

"Mrs Brown, dear. Could you possibly keep an eye on Baby while I go to the shops? I won't be five minutes, I promise. *Don't* put her out in the garden — she seems a bit feverish, poor mite."
"Hello, Baby. Feverish are we? Um, you are a bit hot. Now, what have we got. Coverlet. Two blankets. Oh, and a little light one. And a sheet. And what about you? Let's look. Yes, I know you like being tickled. You are a nice baby. Cardigan. Babygro. Vest. Plastic pants. Terry nappy. Liner. Yes — one could say you were feverish. July. Mid morning. And a cardigan. We've got an hour. At the least. Upsy daisy. Let's peel the cardigan. Lose it in the wash. Anyone asks and you were sick on it. Unpop the babygro. Dare I take off the vest? Better not — not this time. But I'll leave the poppers undone. Now, can you fib, Baby? All the bedclothes cunningly hunched to the bottom of the pram. Coverlet back on. You've kicked that lot off, Dear.
"We've got a while yet. No, I don't think we'd better risk the garden — not when she's explicitly said not. But we can open the patio doors. There we are. And we can edge the pram over here, and turn it a bit like this. Now you can see the trees. Look, birds, Baby! Don't you tell her and I'll see what we can do next time. Give it a month and I'll have you out on the lawn. And bare as your birthday if I've got anything to do with it. Now, you lie there and talk to the sparrows while I get on with the ironing. And tell me if you see your mum coming."

Two Hats

"Mind your feet, poppet. Oh, is that for me? *Very* nice. I like
caramel. No, put Dolly over there, love. She can't be very
comfortable on the mat. Look, we'll sit her here where she can
watch. No, I can't read to you, love. I've got to get this floor
done. You read to me. Nonsense, of course you can read. You
tell me what that says. *That's* right CAT. Very good. If you can
read 'cat' you can read *anything*. Look — here's a word —
PLATE. No, not plat. You're very clever to see it's like cat — but
it's got a magic 'e' on the end. What's a magic 'e'? Hasn't teacher
told you? Well . . .
"Oh, it's all right, Mrs Henderson. She's no bother.
I've finished the floor. She can sit here beside me while I iron.
'*Now*. The magic 'e' . . . . . ."

Heaven

A daily woman came to die
- with not a whimper, not a sigh,
for, being Monday, she'd evade
the monumental Tuesday chores
of cleaning drains and parquet floors
- and, Friday, she'd been paid.

Into her pillows snuggled deep
she settled to eternal sleep
but woke to blinding light.
Before her stood St Peter, tall
and stately: "Ah," he said "You heard the call.
Got it exactly right.
Now, first things first - the Pearly Gate
has got into a shocking state
and needs a thorough wash.

The paving, too, is scuffed - the cherubim all drag
their feet. You'll find a pile of rag
down by the garment-issue desk. A touch of Jewellers Rouge, I think
will bring it up a treat. The sink
is blocked in Mansion fifty-four
and would you kindly oil the door
of number eighty five?"
The daily woman sighed,
but pulled herself together
"You'd never know I'm dead!"
she said
"But then, no doubt you get a lot of wear and tear
with such a crowd
treading the golden stair.
Where do you keep your buckets?"
Peter smiled.
"Couldn't resist it - but it isn't fair
to tease . . . For you must understand
the walls are adamantine - never show a scratch
and all the robes are crease-resistant. See
each door and silver latch
is free
of fingermarks
and every floor will shine forever as it does today.
And now
You come along with me.
I've got the kettle on . .
we'll sit and chat awhile
and have a cup of tea."

Daily Woman

I am a daily woman.
Not continuous.
Days are sealed against each other,
acts encapsulated.
My days are dust, detritus of your dream,
the wake of your progression.
Whether of thread or parchment, dust remains dust
and dust I gather and stow safely.

For you, in movement,
I am the steady ticking of a clock
marking a time in which I have no other part.
I follow you only in conjecture.

Never-the-less
time tricks us and leaves all empty handed.
The applause must die
and dust drift down
as the drama is dismantled.
Dust is the only constancy.
For me, an old familiarity.
For you
as inescapable at last.

The Sisterhood

Cleaning woman. Cleaning lady. Char.
The Woman who comes in.
Comes in and takes your place
in the long tradition.
Comes in through your doorway
to scour your dirt away.
Frees you to fly;
but where will you fly?
To type another's words,
to teach another's thoughts.
Come into my mind.
You will find it furnished
very like your own.

Midnight is my Own

Charring and kids and cats devour my day
But midnight is my own.
Between the last chore and the first sleep
I hollow out a place,
line it with words
And peer out at the stars.

OTHER BOOKS FROM EXLEY PUBLICATIONS
For a free colour catalogue of Exley books write to the address below.

What is a Wife?, £3.95. A book for those contemplating, enjoying or
enduring marriage, compiled from the entries of several thousand ordinary
people. The book is a mixture of fun, outraged anger, ribald jokes, and
coming through it all, a great deal of love.

To Mum, £3.95. 'When I'm sad she patches me up with laughter.' A
thoughtful, joyous gift to Mum, entirely created by children. Get it for
Mother's Day or her birthday.

Grandmas and Grandpas, £3.95. Children are close to grandparents, and
this reflects that warmth. "A Grandma is old on the outside and young on the
inside." An endearing book for grandparents, entirely by children.

Help! I've got a Teenager!, £6.95 (hardback). A very helpful book for
parents tearing their hair out because of their teenagers. The authors are
psychologists and joint parents. They offer step-by-step advice on such
problems as what to do if your teenager won't clean his or her room, is
failing at school or is sexually promiscuous.

Is There Life After Housework?, £5.95 (hardback). A revolutionary book
which sets out to show how you can save up to 75% of the time you now
spend on cleaning. It is written by a man who heads one of the largest
cleaning firms in the world. Humorous illustrations throughout. It's a natural
gift to the hardpressed and downtrodden!

For Mother, a gift of love, £4.95. This collection of tributes to mothers in
poetry and prose and illustrated with sensitive grey screened photographs is
bound with a luxurious pale blue suedel cover. Rudyard Kipling, Noël
Coward. T. B. Macaulay, Victor Hugo, Norman Mailer, C. Day Lewis and Alfred
Lord Tennyson are among the contributors. Giftwrapped with sealing wax.

Marriage, a Keepsake, £4.95. Also in the same series, but with a dove-grey
suedel cover. This collection of poems and prose celebrates marriage with
some of the finest love messages between husbands and wives. A gift for all
ages — from those about to be married to those who have known fifty good
years and more together. Giftwrapped with sealing wax.

Ziggy: Plants are some of my favourite people, £2.95. This is a popular
book of Ziggy cartoons. Ziggy is a born loser and his endearing failures make
him appeal to all ages.
Ziggy and his plant have a very special relationship. His plant reacts
emotionally, complains a great deal, gets depressed a lot, is jealous of the
attention Ziggy gives any of his annuals and hates being left alone. A must for
anyone who is potty about plants — or about Ziggy.

Ziggy: Pets are friends who share your rainy days, £2.95. Ziggy's pets
are very special little people who run his life for him. Anyone who has loved
a pet will see themselves in this book.

Ms Murphy's Law, £2.50. If you thought Murphy's Law was hilarious, wait
till you see what Ms Murphy has to say on the subject. She knows only too
well that 'if anything can go wrong it will — and when it does it will be the
woman who has to put it right'. Enchantingly illustrated by Gray Jolliffe's
cartoons.

Books may be ordered through your bookshop, or by post from Exley
Publications, Dept MCI, 16 Chalk Hill, Watford, Herts, United Kingdom WD1
4BN. Please add 60p per book for postage and packing.
Exley Publications reserves the right to show new retail prices on books,
which may differ from those previously advertised.